Simplicity

Simplicity

·Hazelden Encouragements·

Illustrated by
Jody Bishel and Daniel Buckley

The C.R. Gibson Company
Norwalk, Connecticut 06856

Living in the Moment

*Be aware of yourself and validate
your experience. Pay attention to your
world, to what's happening, and why.
...Feel your strength, value it, and use it.*

How do we think or feel in the present?
Take away thoughts of other times and
we may feel lost and confused. It takes time
to learn to live in the present and to trust it.
We need to learn that, for as long as we're in the
present, we exist. We are.

Imagine the moment as a brand new car. All
we need to do is open the door, hop in, and drive
away. For that moment, our thoughts will not be
focused on cars we used to own or on those we're
going to buy in the future. Instead, for that
moment, we are in the here and now. That's how
each of our moments can be: fresh and clean
and exciting.

Tomorrow doesn't matter for
I have lived today.

Horace

The choice to slow down, to honor the flowers,
the children, the loud and silent moment
of our day, is ours.

*The evening star
is the most
beautiful of all stars.*

Sappho

The first star in the evening sky shines with a special brightness, because it is the first. We see it as a signal; the first sign that afternoon has turned to evening.

The first of anything is touched with special glamour; first love, a baby's first words or steps, first day of school, first job. They're signals of change, profound and irreversible. When day turns to evening, that day will never come again. Tomorrow is a new day, unique and never to be repeated.

If we could meet each new day, each new person, each new experience, as though it were the first, our lives could be touched by the excitement and discovery of adventure. We're not the same as we were yesterday. Each moment we change; each new event in our lives can be a cusp between two different states. Today, let's give ourselves that special gift.

*Every moment
is full of wonder
and God is always present.*

Let us be thankful today for all simple obvious things: for the sun's rising this morning without our having to awaken it; for another good turn the earth makes today without expecting anything in return; for our ability to know right and wrong by heart. Let us give thanks for all small things that mean the world to us; for bread and cheese and clean running water; for our ability to call our enemies our friends, to forgive even ourselves; for our own bodies, however sagging and worn, which insist on continuing for at least another day.

*We need to stop
and let the world go on its way
without us once in a while.*

Going With the Flow

You must travel the river, live on it,
follow it when there is morning light, and
follow it when there is nothing but dark
and the banks have blurred into shadows.

Will Haygood

Any lifeguard knows a swimmer who tries to swim against the current stands a good chance of becoming tired and drowning. "Go with the flow" is a good reminder to help us stop going against the current of life.

Sometimes we may discover that our weariness is a result of swimming against today's current. We may have even tried to force changes in people, places or things. We may have even tried to force ourselves to do things we were incapable of doing.

Going with the flow today means accepting the

way we feel—right now. It means listening to our inner voices when they tell us whether we're tired, hungry, cold, or lonely. By accepting ourselves and not fighting how we feel, we'll be better able to travel the river of life.

I remember the story of the old man who said on his deathbed that he had had a lot of trouble in his life, most of which never happened.

Winston Churchill

Life is what it is. It seldom matches our hopes and dreams, but it never fails to be exactly what we need.

Perhaps we are only beginning to realize that there exists a carefully orchestrated plan that each of us has been invited to experience. Our contribution helps to form the plan which enhances our personal development.

We must trust that the plan has our best interests at heart, even though our sights may be focused elsewhere. The evolution of our lives, often in spite of our own misguided efforts, should convince us that we can let go of the reins.

A group of friends went swimming one day and one of them lost a quarter in the bottom of the lake. Everyone started diving from different directions to find it until there was so much mud and sand stirred up that no one could see anything. Finally, they decided to clear the water. They waited silently on the edge of the shore for the mud from their activity to settle. When it finally cleared, one person dove in slowly and picked up the quarter.

When we are confused about something in our lives, we will often hear answers and advice from all directions. Our friends will tell us one thing and our families another, until we feel pretty well mixed up. If we look away from our problem and let patience and time do their work, the mud inside us will settle and clear. Our answer will become visible, like the glimmer of silver in the water.

Muddy water, let stand, becomes clear.

Lao-Tzu

It's human to want to hold on to what's precious. But life's real treasure is found in achieving the rhythm of ebb and flow. Joy can't be a constant state. Glory is part of a cycle that includes defeat.

Accepting imperfection, accepting change, is part of accepting our humanity. We obey the same cyclic laws that govern the universe. Success in living depends on accepting that one day we'll eat cake and the next we won't. Fear tempts us to hoard the crumbs of our success, but wisdom lets us brush them away.

There are as many ways to live and grow as there are people. Our own ways are the only ways that should matter to us.

Evelyn Mandel

We can accept any condition and understand
it as an opportunity to take another step toward
serenity, eternal and whole.

*How much simpler our lives can be
if we have the faith to accept what happens
as a guidepost along a path
that is naturally correct.*

Letting Things Be

May my supper be contentment.
I'll breakfast on hope again tomorrow.

"How much do we need to let go of?" a friend asked one day.

"I'm not certain," I replied, "but maybe everything."

Letting go is a spiritual, emotional, mental, and physical process, a sometimes mysterious metaphysical process of releasing to God and the Universe that which we are clinging to so tightly.

We let go of our grasp on people, outcomes, ideas, feelings, wants, needs, desires— everything.

Letting go is the action part of faith. It is a behavior that gives God and the Universe permission to send us what we're meant to have.

Letting go means we acknowledge that hanging on so tightly isn't helping to solve the problem, change the person, or get the outcome we desire. It isn't helping us. In fact, we learn that hanging on often blocks us from getting what we want and need.

There is magic in letting go. Sometimes we get what we want soon after we let go. Sometimes it takes longer. Sometimes the specific outcome we desire doesn't happen. Something better does.

Letting go sets us free and connects us to our Source.

Letting go creates the optimum environment for the best possible outcomes and solutions.

Melody Beattie

If a button falls off my shirt, I can sew it on again. If I see someone on the street without a button, I can't change the situation. By looking at myself and mending my own fence, I won't be likely to mend others' fences.

You just have to learn not to care about the dust mice under the beds.

Margaret Mead

Don't try to saw sawdust.

Dale Carnegie

*O*nce there was a little girl who was learning to walk. The trouble was, her mother wouldn't let her fall down. Every time she was about to fall, her mother would rush over and catch her.

It was hard to learn how to walk if she couldn't fall down, but the girl was too little to be able to tell her mother. Her mother thought she was taking care of her child when in fact she was keeping her child from learning to take care of herself. Letting her fall would have shown trust in the child, trust that she could get up. It would have taught her child that she wasn't so fragile that she couldn't recover if she hurt herself.

We are all like this mother once in a while, protecting one another from important lessons in life. It's not that we have to let someone get seriously hurt, but that we allow each other the freedom to learn and grow in individual ways.

You want me to succeed so much.

Could you understand if I failed?

Could you love me if I failed?

Sister Mary Paul

It's not easy to let go of someone with whom we want to share a particular path in life; however, no two of us are destined for exactly the same lessons today, or any day. We must each find our own way and develop those opportunities we meet that are certain to enhance the lessons our souls have been created for.

Our need to control someone else generally results from our own insecurities about life's meaning. Because we lack understanding of our personal worth, we look for it in someone else's devotion to us—a devotion that, in time, we squeeze the life from.

We cannot control another's behavior, and yet we try. And the more we try, the greater the barriers between us become.

We cannot force what is not meant to be.

It doesn't matter.

Doesn't matter.

Doesn't matter.

Doesn't matter...

Melody Beattie

Caring For Me

We carry our houseplants from one window
to another to give them the proper
heat, light, air and moisture.
Should we not be at least
as careful of ourselves?

Do I feel anxious and concerned about a responsibility I've been neglecting? Then perhaps I have to let go of my fears and tend to that responsibility.

Do I feel overwhelmed, out of control? Maybe I need to journey back to the first of the Twelve Steps.

Have I been working too hard? Maybe what I need to do is take some time off and do something fun.

Have I been neglecting my work or daily tasks? Then maybe what I need to do is get back to my routine.

There is no recipe, no formula, no guidebook

for self-care. We each have a guide, and that guide is within us. We need to ask the question: 'What do I need to do to take loving, responsible care of myself?' Then, we need to listen to the answer. Self-care is not that difficult. The most challenging part is trusting the answer, and having the courage to follow through once we hear it.

Melody Beattie

When someone tells us we should do something, do we want to do it, or do we feel mad that someone else is telling us what we want to do? Sometimes we forget that these messages are not our own, but are the desires of others. It's important to listen to what we tell ourselves, to be aware of which messages we're giving ourselves and which come from others.

We can make a list of all our shoulds and identify where they came from: parent, boss, friend, self. Then we can decide which shoulds are want tos, and throw out the rest. Doing what we want to is very different from doing what we should, and we can usually do a better job of it.

Today I'll remember that I'm all I need to be.

You didn't cause it;

you can't control it;

and you can't cure it.

I can't be all things
to all people
if I'm to be the person
I need to be for me.

*T*hree women were talking. One blamed herself for an unkind remark someone had made to her. Another blamed herself for not getting work done. The other compared her looks to those of the movie stars and thought she was ugly.

The women each noticed how the other two had put themselves down. They vowed then to be as kind to themselves as they were to each other. Each time they caught themselves being mean to themselves, they imagined they were their own best friend, and tried to be as understanding of themselves as they were to one another.

When we are kind to ourselves, only then can we be truly kind to others, and make ourselves a gift to those around us.

Self-love makes me vulnerable and compassionate towards others. It's the balm for all wounds; it multiplies as it's expressed. It can begin with my smile.

A variation on the Golden Rule:
Do unto ourselves
as we would have others
do unto us.

When will we become lovable?
When will we feel safe? When will we get
all the protection, nurturing and love we richly
deserve? We will get it when we begin
giving it to ourselves.

Melody Beattie

We've been invited to participate in this life, to be present, one for another, and that's all that's expected of us.

Colophon

Compiled and edited by Stephanie C. Oda
Designed by Aurora Campanella Lyman
Calligraphed by Martin Holloway
Type set in Kunstler Script, Bodoni Book Italic